Connected Mathematics™

What Do You Expect?

Probability and Expected Value

Student Edition

Glenda Lappan
James T. Fey
William M. Fitzgerald
Susan N. Friel
Elizabeth Difanis Phillips

Prentice Hall

Glenview, Illinois
Needham, Massachusetts
Upper Saddle River, New Jersey

Connected Mathematics™ was developed at Michigan State University with the support of National Science Foundation Grant No. MDR 9150217.

This project was supported, in part,
by the
National Science Foundation
Opinions expressed are those of the authors
and not necessarily those of the Foundation

The Michigan State University authors and administration have agreed that all MSU royalties arising from this publication will be devoted to purposes supported by the Department of Mathematics and the MSU Mathematics Education Enrichment Fund.

Photo Acknowledgements: 27 © William Carter/Photo Researchers, Inc.; 29 © Mitch Wojnarowicz/The Image Works; 33 © Topham/The Image Works; 34 © Peter Menzel/Stock, Boston; 47 © James Carroll/Stock, Boston; 50 © Carl Sissac/Sports Illustrated; 54 © Shelley Gazin/The Image Works; 56 © Mitch Wojnarowicz/The Image Works; 57 © Bob Daemmrich/Stock, Boston; 61 © Tim Davis/Photo Researchers, Inc.; 69 © Renee Lynn/Photo Researchers, Inc.; 74 © Fred Lion/Rapho/Photo Researchers, Inc.

Prentice
Hall

ISBN 0-13-053074-3

1 2 3 4 5 6 7 8 9 10   05 04 03 02 01

The Connected Mathematics Project Staff

Project Directors

James T. Fey
University of Maryland

William M. Fitzgerald
Michigan State University

Susan N. Friel
University of North Carolina at Chapel Hill

Glenda Lappan
Michigan State University

Elizabeth Difanis Phillips
Michigan State University

Project Manager

Kathy Burgis
Michigan State University

Technical Coordinator

Judith Martus Miller
Michigan State University

Curriculum Development Consultants

David Ben-Chaim
Weizmann Institute

Alex Friedlander
Weizmann Institute

Eleanor Geiger
University of Maryland

Jane Mitchell
University of North Carolina at Chapel Hill

Anthony D. Rickard
Alma College

Collaborating Teachers/Writers

Mary K. Bouck
Portland, Michigan

Jacqueline Stewart
Okemos, Michigan

Graduate Assistants

Scott J. Baldridge
Michigan State University

Angie S. Eshelman
Michigan State University

M. Faaiz Gierdien
Michigan State University

Jane M. Keiser
Indiana University

Angela S. Krebs
Michigan State University

James M. Larson
Michigan State University

Ronald Preston
Indiana University

Tat Ming Sze
Michigan State University

Sarah Theule-Lubienski
Michigan State University

Jeffrey J. Wanko
Michigan State University

Evaluation Team

Mark Hoover
Michigan State University

Diane V. Lambdin
Indiana University

Sandra K. Wilcox
Michigan State University

Judith S. Zawojewski
National-Louis University

Teacher/Assessment Team

Kathy Booth
Waverly, Michigan

Anita Clark
Marshall, Michigan

Julie Faulkner
Traverse City, Michigan

Theodore Gardella
Bloomfield Hills, Michigan

Yvonne Grant
Portland, Michigan

Linda R. Lobue
Vista, California

Suzanne McGrath
Chula Vista, California

Nancy McIntyre
Troy, Michigan

Mary Beth Schmitt
Traverse City, Michigan

Linda Walker
Tallahassee, Florida

Software Developer

Richard Burgis
East Lansing, Michigan

Development Center Directors

Nicholas Branca
San Diego State University

Dianne Briars
Pittsburgh Public Schools

Frances R. Curcio
New York University

Perry Lanier
Michigan State University

J. Michael Shaughnessy
Portland State University

Charles Vonder Embse
Central Michigan University

Special thanks to the students and teachers at these pilot schools!

Contents

What Do You Expect?

In the district finals, Nicky has just been fouled and is in a one-and-one free-throw situation. This means that she must make her first shot to try a second shot. Nicky's free-throw average is 60%. Is Nicky most likely to miss the first shot, to make the first shot and miss the second shot, or to make both shots?

Raymundo invented the Prime Number Multiplication game. Two 1-6 number cubes are rolled to get a product. Player A scores 10 points if the product is prime, and Player B scores 1 point if it is not prime. Raymundo thinks his game is fair because there are many more ways to roll a nonprime product than a prime product. Is his game a fair game?

Have you ever had to guess because you forgot to study for a quiz? If you take a five-question true-false quiz and guess on every question, what are your chances of getting every question right?

Probabilities can help you make decisions. For example, if the weather report says there is a 75% chance of rain, you might decide to carry an umbrella. If you know there is a 1 in 1,000,000 chance of winning the lottery, you might choose not to play. Probabilities can also help you predict what will happen over the long run. For example, if you and your friend flip a coin before each baseball game to determine who will be catcher, you can predict that you will be catcher for about half the games.

Many probability situations involve some kind of payoff—points scored in a game, money won in a lottery, or profit earned from a business venture. It is often useful to find the long-term average payoff, or the *expected value*, in situations like these. For example, when deciding whether to make an investment, a company might want to figure out how much it can expect to earn over the long run.

In this unit, you will look at questions involving probability and expected value, including the three questions on the opposite page.

Mathematical Highlights

In *What Do You Expect?* you will explore ways to deepen your understanding of basic probability concepts and learn about the expected value of chance situations. This unit will help you to

- Understand experimental and theoretical probabilities and the relationship between them;

- Further develop ways to identify the possible outcomes of an event;

- Understand the distinction between equally likely and non–equally likely events;

- Analyze situations that involve independent events and situations that involve dependent events;

- Develop a variety of strategies for analyzing probabilities, such as using lists, counting trees and area models;

- Determine the expected value of a chance situation; and

- Use probability and expected value to make decisions.

As you work on the problems in this unit, ask yourself questions about situations that involve analyzing probabilities: *What are the possible outcomes for the event(s) in this situation? Are they equally likely? Can I compute the theoretical probabilities or do I need to find experimental probabilities associated with the outcomes of the event(s)? If I'm exploring two or more events, are they independent or dependent events? In the context of games, how can I use expected value to help me determine whether a game is fair or unfair?*

Evaluating Games of Chance

In this investigation, you will explore several games involving chance. In each situation, you are asked to determine the chance, or *probability*, that certain outcomes will occur. In some situations, you will also be asked to determine whether a particular game is fair. What do you think it means for a game to be fair?

1.1 What's in the Bucket?

One day, Ms. MacAfee brought a mysterious bucket to class. She did not show her students what was in the bucket, but she told them that it contained blue, yellow, and red blocks. She asked if they could predict, without emptying the bucket, the fraction of the blocks that were blue, the fraction that were yellow, and the fraction that were red.

The class conducted an experiment to help them make their predictions. Each student randomly selected a block from the bucket, and the result was recorded on the board. After each draw, the block was returned to the bucket before the next student selected a block. In this problem, your class will conduct a similar experiment.

Problem 1.1

Your teacher has prepared a bucket identical to Ms. MacAfee's. One at a time, you and each of your classmates will select a block from the bucket, record the result, and return the block to the bucket.

A. How many blocks drawn by your class were blue? How many were yellow? How many were red?

B. Which color block—blue, yellow, or red—do you think there are the greatest number of in the bucket? Which color block do you think there are the least number of?

C. Based on your experimental data, predict the fraction of blocks in the bucket that are blue, that are yellow, and that are red.

D. After your teacher shows you the blocks in the bucket, find the fraction of blue blocks, the fraction of yellow blocks, and the fraction of red blocks.

E. How do the fractions of blocks that are blue, yellow, and red compare to the fractions of blue, yellow, and red blocks drawn during the experiment?

■ Problem 1.1 Follow-Up

1. a. Is each block *equally likely* to be selected from the bucket? That is, does each block have the same chance of being selected? Explain your reasoning.

  b. Is each color equally likely to be selected? Explain your reasoning.

2. What is the probability of drawing a white block from the bucket?

3. How many blue blocks need to be added to the bucket for the probability of drawing a blue block to be $\frac{1}{2}$?

1.2 Matching Colors

April and Tioko invented a two-player spinner game called Match/No-Match. A player spins this spinner twice on his or her turn. If both spins land on the same color (a match), Player A scores. If the two spins land on different colors (a no-match), Player B scores. Since there are two matching combinations—blue/blue and yellow/yellow—they decided that Player A should score only 1 point for a match and Player B should score 2 points for a no-match.

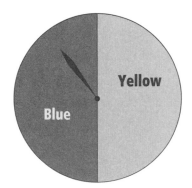

Problem 1.2

Play the Match/No-Match game with a partner. Take a total of 24 turns (12 turns for each player). For each turn, record the color pair on Labsheet 1.2, and award points to the appropriate player.

A. Use the results you collected to find the *experimental probabilities* of a match and a no-match. The experimental probability of a match is

$$P(\text{match}) = \frac{\text{number of turns that are matches}}{\text{total number of turns}}$$

The experimental probability of a no-match is

$$P(\text{no-match}) = \frac{\text{number of turns that are no-matches}}{\text{total number of turns}}$$

B. List all the possible **outcomes** of a turn (two spins). Write the outcomes as pairs of the form *color on first spin / color on second spin,* such as blue/blue. Use your list to determine the *theoretical probabilities* of a match and a no-match. Since all the outcomes are equally likely, the theoretical probability of a match is

$$P(\text{match}) = \frac{\text{number of outcomes that are matches}}{\text{number of possible outcomes}}$$

The theoretical probability of a no-match is

$$P(\text{no-match}) = \frac{\text{number of outcomes that are no-matches}}{\text{number of possible outcomes}}$$

C. How do your results for parts A and B compare?

D. Is Match/No-Match a **fair game**? If you think the game is fair, explain why. If you think it is not fair, explain how the rules could be changed to make it fair.

■ **Problem 1.2 Follow-Up**

1. Are a match and a no-match equally likely? Explain your reasoning.
2. In 100 turns of the Match/No-Match game, how many times would you expect each of the following to occur?
   a. two yellows
   b. two blues
   c. one yellow and one blue
   d. at least one yellow

3. a. Look at your results on Labsheet 1.2. If you had stopped after one turn, what would have been the experimental probability of a match? If you had stopped after two turns, what would have been the experimental probability of a match? If you had stopped after three turns, what would have been the experimental probability of a match? Continue to find the experimental probabilities through 24 turns. Record your results in a table.

b. Plot your data from part a on a coordinate grid similar to the one below.

c. What do you think your graph would look like if you had taken 30 turns? 50 turns? 100 turns? 1000 turns?

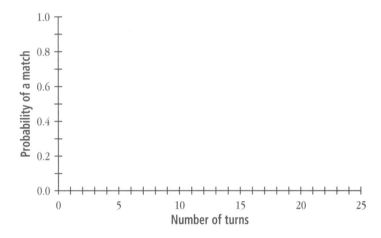

1.3 Making Purple

The most popular game at the school carnival is a spinner game called Making Purple. To play the game, a player spins each of the spinners below once. If the player gets red on spinner A and blue on spinner B, the player wins, because red and blue together make purple.

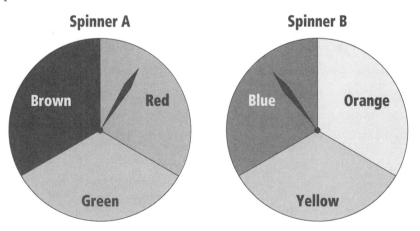

Problem 1.3

A. Play Making Purple 50 times, and record the results on Labsheet 1.3. Based on your results, what is the experimental probability that a player will "make purple" on any single turn?

B. Plot the experimental probability of making purple you would have found if you had stopped after 5 turns, 10 turns, 15 turns, and so on, up to 50 turns.

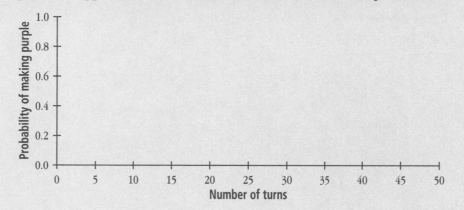

C. What do you think your graph would look like if you had taken 100 turns? 200 turns? 1000 turns?

D. List the possible outcomes for a turn. Write the outcomes as pairs of the form *color on spinner A/color on spinner B*. Are the outcomes equally likely? Explain why or why not.

E. What is the theoretical probability that a player will make purple on a turn?

F. How does the experimental probability of making purple compare with the theoretical probability of making purple? Explain.

■ Problem 1.3 Follow-Up

1. If 36 people play this game, how many would you expect to win? Explain how you got your answer.

2. Tickets at the school carnival cost 50¢ each. It takes four tickets to play the Making Purple game. The prizes awarded to the winners cost the school $5 each. Suppose 36 people play the game.
  a. How much money will the school take in from this game?
  b. How much money would you expect the school to pay out in prizes?
  c. How much profit would you expect the school to make from this game?

You can find all the possible outcomes of a situation
by making an organized list. Creating a **counting tree**
can help you make sure you find all the possibilities.
April used a counting tree to show all the possible
outcomes for the Match/No-Match game (from
Problem 1.2). First, she listed the equally likely
outcomes of the first spin as shown in the tree
at right below.

1, 2, 3

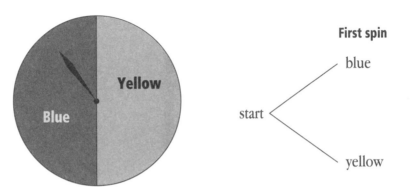

A turn consists of two spins, so from each of the possible results of the first spin, April
drew two branches and labeled them to show the possible results of the second spin.

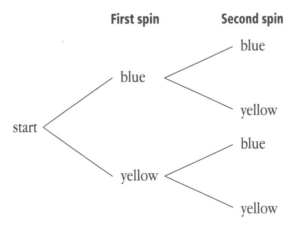

By following the paths from left to right, April can read all the possible outcomes of
a turn. For example, she can follow the upper branch from start to blue, and then from
there follow the upper branch to blue. This path represents the outcome blue/blue.

The column to the right of the tree below lists the possible outcomes.

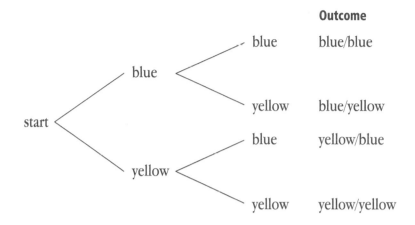

Outcome

blue   blue/blue

blue

yellow   blue/yellow

start

blue   yellow/blue

yellow

yellow   yellow/yellow

Problem 1.4

April and Tioko decide to play the Match/No-Match game on the spinner below. As in the original game, a turn consists of two spins. Player A scores 1 point if the spins match, and Player B scores 1 point if they do not match.

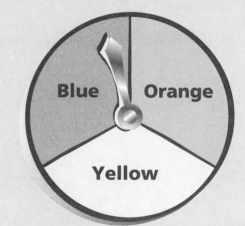

A. Use a counting tree to find all the possible outcomes for this game.

B. What is the theoretical probability of getting a match on a turn?

C. What is the theoretical probability of getting a no-match on a turn?

D. Do you think this is a fair game? If you think the game is fair, explain why. If you think it is not fair, explain how the rules could be changed to make it fair.

1. a. Find all the possible outcomes for the Making Purple game in Problem 1.3 by creating a counting tree.

    b. Use your counting tree to find the theoretical probability of making purple on a turn.

    c. How does the theoretical probability you found by using a counting tree compare with the theoretical probability you found in Problem 1.3?

2. Shondra played a game with a spinner and a coin. For each turn, she spun the spinner once and tossed the coin once. For example, one possible outcome would be blue/head.

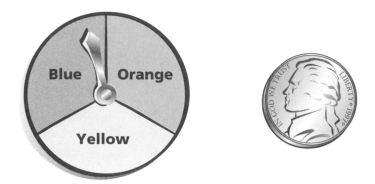

    a. Create a counting tree to find all the possible outcomes of a turn in Shondra's game.

    b. Are all the outcomes equally likely? Explain why or why not.

    c. What is the probability that Shondra will spin blue and toss a head on a turn?

As you work on these ACE questions, use your calculator whenever you need it.

Applications

In 1–5, decide whether the possible resulting events are equally likely, and briefly explain your answer.

Action	Possible resulting events
1. You roll a number cube.	You roll an even number, or you roll an odd number.
2. A baby is born.	The baby is left-handed, or the baby is right-handed.
3. You toss a marshmallow.	The marshmallow lands on its end, or the marshmallow lands on its side.
4. You draw a card from a standard deck of 52 playing cards with no jokers.	The card is a heart, the card is a club, the card is a diamond, or the card is a spade.
5. You toss a coin three times.	You get three heads, you get two heads and a tail, you get a head and two tails, or you get three tails.

6. The probability of an event is a number between 0 and 1. The greater the probability, the greater the chances the event will happen. If an event is impossible, the probability that it will occur is 0, or 0%. If an event is certain to happen, the probability that it will occur is 1, or 100%.

Copy the number line below. Place the letter of each event below on the number line at the spot that best describes its probability.

a. You will get a head when you toss a coin.

b. You can run 20 miles in one hour.

c. You will roll a 6 on a number cube.

d. It will snow in Minnesota this winter.

e. The sun will rise tomorrow.

f. You will toss a coin twice and get two heads.

g. You will toss a coin twice and get at least one head.

h. You will listen to a CD today.

i. You will spin the spinner shown below once, and it will land on red.

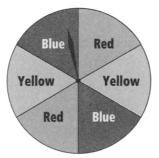

7. Lori's little sister Lulu tore the labels from ten cans of vegetables. Now all of the cans look exactly the same. Lori knows that three of the cans contain corn, two contain spinach, four contain beans, and one contains tomatoes. Lori picks a can at random and opens it.

   a. What is the probability that the can contains corn?

   b. What is the probability that the can contains beans?

   c. What is the probability that the can does *not* contain spinach?

   d. What is the probability that the can contains beans or tomatoes?

   e. Is it equally likely that any one of the vegetables is in the can? Explain.

8. If a tack is dropped on the floor, there are two possible outcomes: the tack lands on its side (point down), or the tack lands on its head (point up). The probability that a tack will land point up or point down can be determined by experimenting. Kalifa tossed a tack 100 times and recorded the results in the table below.

point down   point up

Outcome	Number of times it occurs
Tack lands point up	58
Tack lands point down	42

   a. If you dropped Kalifa's tack once, what is the probability that it would land point up? What is the probability that it would land point down?

   b. If you dropped Kalifa's tack 500 times, how many times would you expect it to land point up?

   c. Is it equally likely that the tack will land point up or point down? Explain.

   d. Is it possible to determine theoretical probabilities for this situation? Why or why not?

9. José is going to a party. He has decided to wear his jeans and a sweater, but he can't decide what else to wear. The counting tree below shows the possible outfits he can make if he randomly selects sneakers or loafers; blue, red, or brown socks; and a black, red, or plaid cap.

a. What are the chances that José will wear loafers, blue socks, and a plaid cap?

b. What are the chances that José will wear sneakers, either red or blue socks, and a black cap?

c. What are the chances that José will wear neither red socks nor a red cap?

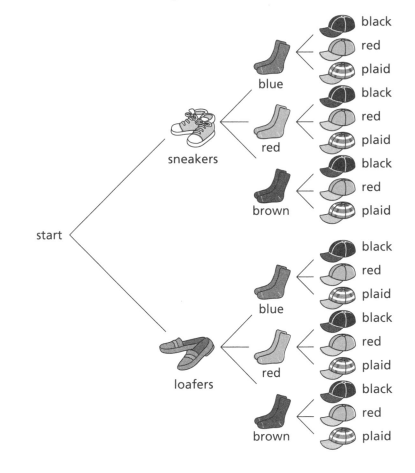

10. Tino and Kim are playing a game with two pennies. The players take turns tossing both pennies. If the pennies match, Tino scores 1 point. If they don't match, Kim scores 1 point.

    a. Is this a fair game? Explain.

    b. How does this game compare to the Match/No-Match game in Problem 1.2?

    c. Kim suggests playing the game with three pennies instead of two. The rules would be the same—Tino would get a point if the three pennies matched, and Kim would get a point if they didn't all match. Is this a fair game? Why or why not?

11. In the Gee Whiz Everyone Wins! television game show, members of the studio audience draw a block randomly from the bucket shown at right. If a blue block is drawn, the contestant wins $5. If a red block is drawn, the contestant wins $10. If the yellow block is drawn, the contestant wins $50. The block is replaced after each draw.

    a. What is the probability of drawing each color?

    b. If 24 contestants draw a block from the bucket, how much money can the game show expect to pay out?

12. At the school carnival, the Math Club is running a coin-toss game. It costs four 50¢ tickets to play the game. A player tosses two coins. If the coins match, the player wins a prize. Each prize costs the club $5. Can the club expect to make a profit on this game? If so, how much? If not, explain why.

13. Tioko and Dione are using the spinners from the Making Purple game to play a two-person game. They take turns spinning the two spinners. If the colors on the two spinners make purple, Dione scores. If they do not make purple, Tioko scores. For this to be a fair game, how many points should Dione score when the spinners make purple, and how many points should Tioko score when they do not make purplc?

14. Suppose the spinners for the Making Purple game were changed to the following.

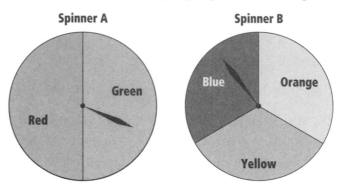

Spinner A   Spinner B

    a. Make a counting tree, and list all the possible outcomes for this game.

    b. Find the theoretical probability of making purple on a turn.

Connections

15. A dart is thrown at random at each of the dartboards below.

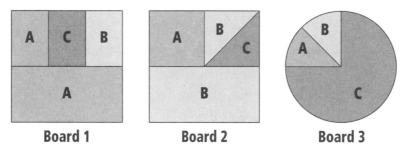

    Board 1   Board 2   Board 3

    a. For each dartboard, what is the probability that a dart will land in a region marked A? A region marked B? A region marked C?

    b. For board 1, what is the probability that a dart will land in a region marked A or B?

    c. For board 2, what is the probability that a dart will *not* land in region C?

16. A dartboard is divided into four regions, A, B, C, and D. The probability that a randomly thrown dart will land in region A is 40%. The probabilities that the dart will land in region B, region C, or region D are all equal.

   a. What is the probability that a dart will land in a region other than A?

   b. Make a square dartboard that meets the given conditions.

   c. Make a circular dartboard that meets the given conditions.

17. Jason spins the spinner below several times and tallies the results in a table.

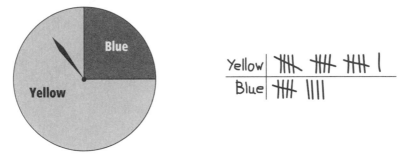

   a. How many times did Jason spin the spinner?

   b. What percent of the spins landed in the blue region? In the yellow region?

   c. According to the theoretical probabilities, what percent of the spins should land in the blue region? In the yellow region?

   d. Compare the experimental probability of the spinner landing in each region with the theoretical probability. If the probabilities are different, explain why.

Extensions

18. A bucket contains 60 marbles—some red, some blue, and some white. The probability of drawing a red marble is 35%, and the probability of drawing a blue marble is 25%. How many marbles of each color are in the bucket?

19. Hannah's teacher brought in a bucket containing 72 blocks—some red, some yellow, and some blue. Hannah wanted to try to figure out how many of the blocks were blue without emptying the bucket. She drew a block from the bucket, recorded its color, and then replaced it. She did this 14 times. Of her 14 draws, 5 were blue. Based on Hannah's experiment, how many of the blocks are blue? Explain your answer.

20. All the winners from the Gee Whiz Everyone Wins! game show get an opportunity to compete for a bonus prize. Each contestant draws one block at random from each of the buckets shown below. If the blocks are the same color, the contestant wins a prize.

Bucket 1   Bucket 2

a. List all the possible outcomes when a player randomly draws one block from each bucket.

b. What is the probability that a contestant will draw two blocks of the same color?

c. Natasha wants to use a similar game at the school carnival. Contestants would pay two 50¢ tickets to play and would win a prize worth $3 for a match. Could the school expect to make money from this game? Explain.

Mathematical Reflections

In this investigation, you explored games of chance. Working on the problems gave you an opportunity to review ideas about experimental probability and theoretical probability. These questions will help you summarize what you have learned:

1 **a.** Write a brief description of experimental probability.

   b. Describe a strategy you have used to find experimental probabilities.

2 **a.** Write a brief description of theoretical probability.

   b. Describe strategies you have used to find theoretical probabilities.

3 What does it mean for two or more events to be equally likely? Give examples of events that are equally likely.

Think about your answers to these questions, discuss your ideas with other students and your teacher, and then write a summary of your findings in your journal.

Analyzing Number-Cube Games

In Investigation 1, you used various strategies to find probabilities associated with games of chance. You found *experimental probabilities* by playing a game several times and evaluating the results, and you found *theoretical probabilities* by analyzing the possible outcomes of a game. In this investigation, you will explore experimental and theoretical probabilities involved in some number-cube games.

2.1 Playing the Addition Game

In this problem, you will play the Addition Game with a partner and try to determine whether it is fair.

Addition Game Rules

- Player A and Player B take turns rolling two number cubes.
- If the sum of the numbers rolled is odd, Player A scores 1 point.
- If the sum of the numbers rolled is even, Player B scores 1 point.
- The player with the most points after 36 rolls wins.

Problem 2.1

Play the Addition Game with a partner. Keep track of your results.

A. Based on your data, what is the experimental probability of rolling an odd sum? An even sum?

B. List all the possible pairs of numbers you can roll with two number cubes.

C. What is the theoretical probability of rolling an odd sum? An even sum?

D. Do you think the Addition Game is a fair game? Explain why or why not.

Problem 2.1 Follow-Up

1. Min-wei invented a game based on the sum of two number cubes. In her game, Player A scores 1 point for sums of 6 or 7, and Player B scores 1 point for any other sum. Min-wei thought this would be a fair game because sums of 6 and 7 occur so often. Is this a fair game? Explain why or why not.

2. Royce invented a game based on the sum of two number cubes. In his game, Player A scores 3 points if the sum is a multiple of 3, and Player B scores 1 point if the sum is *not* a multiple of 3. Is Royce's game a fair game? Explain why or why not.

2.2 Playing the Multiplication Game

In the Addition Game, players score points based on the sum of the numbers rolled on two number cubes. In the Multiplication Game, scoring depends on the *product* of the numbers rolled.

Multiplication Game Rules
- Player A and Player B take turns rolling two number cubes.
- If the product of the numbers rolled is odd, Player A scores 1 point.
- If the product of the numbers rolled is even, Player B scores 1 point.
- The player with the most points after 36 rolls wins.

Problem 2.2

Play the Multiplication Game with a partner. Keep track of your results.

A. Based on your data, what is the experimental probability of rolling an odd product? An even product?

B. What is the theoretical probability of rolling an odd product? An even product?

C. Do you think the Multiplication Game is fair? Explain why or why not.

D. If the game consisted of 100 rolls instead of 36, how many points would you expect each player to have at the end of the game?

■ **Problem 2.2 Follow-Up**

1. How could you make the Multiplication Game a fair game?
2. Invent a fair two-person game based on the product of two number cubes. A player should score 1 point each time he or she scores. You will need to decide which player scores on which kinds of products. Explain why your game is fair.

As you work on these ACE questions, use your calculator whenever you need it.

Applications

In 1–4, find the probability of getting the given result when two number cubes are rolled.

1. a sum of 4

2. a sum less than 6

3. a sum of 7 or 11

4. a pair of 5s

5. Suppose you were to spin the spinner below and then roll a number cube.

a. Make an organized list of the possible outcomes.

b. What is the probability that you will get a 1 on both the number cube and the spinner?

c. What is the probability that you will *not* get a 1 on both the number cube and the spinner?

d. What is the probability that you will get a 1 on the number cube or the spinner?

e. What is the probability that you will get the same number on the number cube and the spinner?

f. What is the probability that the sum of the number on the spinner and the number on the number cube will be greater than 8?

g. What is the probability that the product of the number on the spinner and the number on the number cube will be 0?

6. Chris did an experiment using the spinner and number cube from question 5. For each trial, he spun the spinner and then rolled the number cube. He was surprised to find that he got a 1 on both the spinner and the number cube in 4 out of 36 trials.

a. Based on his results, what is the experimental probability of getting a 1 on both the number cube and the spinner?

b. Chris compared the experimental probability of getting a 1 on both the number cube and the spinner to the theoretical probability. He decided that something must be wrong with the spinner or the number cube, since these probabilities are not the same. Do you agree? Why or why not?

7. Raymundo invented the Prime Number Multiplication game. In this game, two number cubes are rolled. Player A scores 10 points if the product is prime, and Player B scores 1 point if the product is not prime. Raymundo thinks this scoring system is reasonable because there are many more ways to roll a nonprime product than a prime product.

a. If the cubes are rolled 100 times, how many points would you expect Player A to score? How many points would you expect Player B to score?

b. Is Raymundo's game a fair game? Explain why or why not.

8. Rachel says that if she rolls two number cubes 36 times, she will get a product of 1 exactly once. Luis said that she cannot be sure this will happen exactly once, but it will probably happen very few times. Who is right? Explain your reasoning.

9. Rachel told Luis that if she rolls two number cubes 100 times, she will *never* get a product of 23. Luis told her that she can't be sure. Who is right? Explain your reasoning.

10. Juanita is trying to decide whether to play a certain game at an amusement park. It takes one ticket to play the game. A player flips two plastic bottles. If both bottles land standing up, the player wins ten tickets to use for rides and games. Juanita has been watching people play the game for a while and has recorded the results in a table:

Both land on side	One lands on side and one lands standing up	Both land standing up
ɪɪɪɪ ɪɪɪɪ ɪɪɪɪ ɪɪɪɪ ɪɪɪɪ ɪɪɪɪ ɪɪɪɪ	ɪɪɪɪ ɪɪɪɪ ɪɪɪɪ	ɪɪ

a. Based on Juanita's results, what is the experimental probability of winning the game?

b. If Juanita played this game 20 times, how many times could she expect to win?

c. How many tickets could Juanita expect to be ahead or behind after playing the game 20 times? Explain your reasoning.

d. Is it possible to find the theoretical probability of winning this game? Why or why not?

In 11–15, tell whether theoretical or experimental probability is being used.

11. Kelly played darts on a board made of concentric blue, red, and yellow regions. The dart landed in the red region 7 times and in the other regions a total of 13 times. Kelly stated that on her next throw, the dart has a 35% chance of landing in the red region.

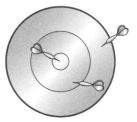

12. For 10 minutes before school each day, some students from Ms. MacAfee's class recorded the types of vehicles that passed by the school. They wanted to figure out whether it was more likely for a car or a truck to pass by. After a week of observing, the students used their data to predict that a car is more likely to pass by than a truck.

13. Emma is in the fun house at the amusement park. She must choose from among three exits. At one exit, visitors get squirted with water. At another exit, visitors get sprayed with whipped cream. At a third exit, visitors must walk through mud. Emma does not know which exit is which. She decides that if she selects an exit at random, she has a $\frac{1}{3}$ chance of getting sprayed with whipped cream.

14. Waldo buys a pair of weighted number cubes at a novelty store. In 30 rolls, he gets a sum of 2 eleven times. Waldo figures that if he rolls the number cubes 100 times, he will get a sum of 2 about 37 times.

15. Tina keeps a pack of 20 colored pencils in her backpack. When her science teacher asks the students to design a cover for their science projects, Tina pulls out a colored pencil without looking. She figures she has about a 5% chance of picking her favorite color, orange.

Connections

16. Marinda and Isaiah are analyzing a game involving two different spinners. For each turn, a player spins each spinner once. To help them find theoretical probabilities, Marinda and Isaiah made the counting tree at right.

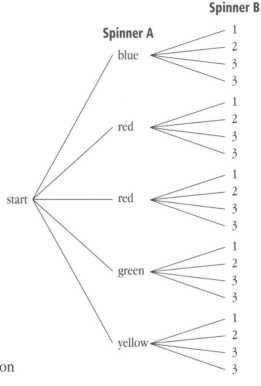

a. Design two spinners that could be the spinners used by Marinda and Isaiah.

b. List all the possible outcomes of spinning each spinner once.

c. Which color/number combination has the greatest probability of occurring?

d. Based on your spinners, what is the probability of getting red on spinner A and 3 on spinner B?

e. Based on your spinners, what is the probability of *not* getting 3 on spinner B?

17. a. When you roll two number cubes, what is the probability that the product of the numbers will be a multiple of 5?

b. If you roll two number cubes 100 times, about how many times can you expect the product to be a multiple of 5?

c. What is the probability of rolling a product that is a multiple of 7?

d. If you roll two number cubes a million times, how many times can you expect to get a product that is a multiple of 7?

18. David went to Miceli's Deli for lunch. He saw the sign below:

> # Sandwich Special:
> choose 1 bread, 1 meat, and 1 cheese — $1.79
>
> ⬜ Breads   🍖 Meats   △ Cheeses
>
> Rye   Turkey   Swiss
> White   Ham   Cheddar
>   Salami   Mozzarella

David couldn't decide which kind of sandwich he wanted, so he told the sandwich maker to surprise him. If the sandwich maker chooses the bread, meat, and cheese at random, what is the probability that David will get a turkey sandwich on wheat bread with cheddar cheese? Explain your reasoning.

19. Tricia wants to determine the probability of getting two 1s when two number cubes are rolled. She made a counting tree and used it to list the possible outcomes.

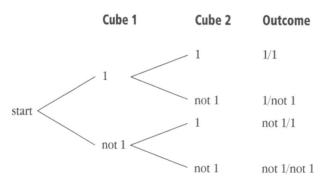

Cube 1	Cube 2	Outcome
1	1	1/1
	not 1	1/not 1
not 1	1	not 1/1
	not 1	not 1/not 1

She says that, since there are four possible outcomes, the probability of getting 1 on both number cubes is $\frac{1}{4}$. Is Tricia right? Why or why not?

20. The authors of this book surveyed middle school students from several schools across the country to try to determine what interests middle school students. One question they asked was: "How interested are you in bicycling?" The bar graphs below show the results for 44 girls and 42 boys.

Interest in Bicycling

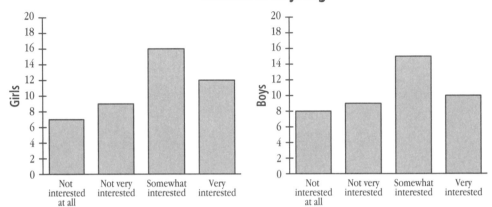

a. Based on the results of the survey, what is the probability that a middle school girl will say she is very interested in bicycling?

b. Based on the results of the survey, what is the probability that a middle school boy will say he is very interested in bicycling?

Extensions

21. Make up a fair game that involves tossing three coins. Describe the rules of your game, and explain why your game is fair.

22. When you roll three number cubes, what is the probability that all three numbers will match?

23. When you roll three number cubes, what is the probability that the product of the numbers will be greater than 200?

24. Matthew invented a two-person game in which players take turns rolling three number cubes. If the sum is even, Player A scores 1 point. If the sum is odd, Player B scores 1 point. Is Matthew's game a fair game? Explain why or why not.

Mathematical Reflections

In this investigation, you looked at games involving number cubes. You determined whether games were fair and figured out how you could change the rules of an unfair game to make it a fair game. These questions will help you summarize what you have learned:

1. What does it mean for a game of chance to be fair?

2. Create a game that is not fair. How can you adjust the system of scoring to make the game fair?

3. In a game of chance, how can you predict the number of times out of 100 a certain outcome will occur? Give an example if it helps you to explain your thinking.

Think about your answers to these questions, discuss your ideas with other students and your teacher, and then write a summary of your findings in your journal.

Probability and Area

In this investigation, you will explore a computer game called Treasure Hunt, which involves searching for treasure in a royal palace. You will see how you can use theoretical probability to improve your chances of winning the game.

3.1 Cracking Level 1

When you play the first level of the Treasure Hunt game, the computer hides a treasure on the first floor of the palace. The floor plan is pictured here.

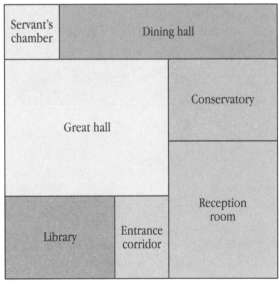

Level 1

The computer gives the player clues about where the treasure is located. After each clue, the player must guess which room the treasure is in. The computer continues to give clues until the player finds the treasure. The fewer clues the player needs to find the treasure, the more points the player gets.

To make good guesses when playing Treasure Hunt, it helps to understand how the computer hides the treasure. The computer "thinks" of the first floor of the palace as a 10 by 10 grid. At the start of a game, the computer **randomly** selects one of the 100 squares as the location for the treasure. For example, if the computer selects the square indicated on the left grid below, the treasure is hidden in the conservatory.

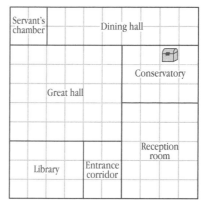

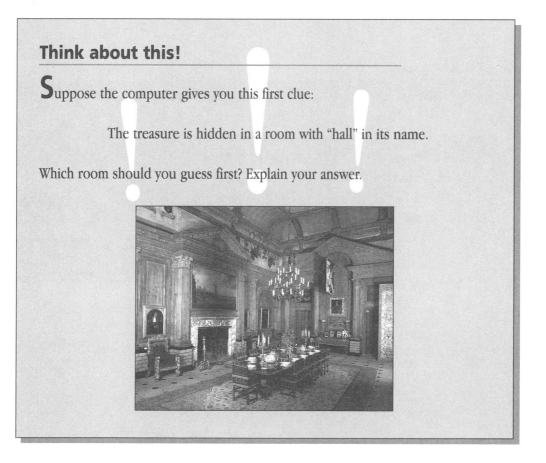

Think about this!

Suppose the computer gives you this first clue:

The treasure is hidden in a room with "hall" in its name.

Which room should you guess first? Explain your answer.

Problem 3.1

A. How can this information about how the computer hides the treasure help you find the treasure?

B. You have just entered level 1 of Treasure Hunt. What is the probability that the treasure is hidden in the great hall? In the servant's chamber?

C. If you play level 1 ten times, how many times can you expect the treasure to be hidden in the great hall? In the servant's chamber?

■ Problem 3.1 Follow-Up

1. The first time you play level 1, the treasure is hidden in the library. What is the probability that the treasure will be hidden in the library the second time you play level 1?

2. Monty says that since the computer randomly picks the location of the treasure, the treasure is just as likely to be hidden in the entrance corridor as in the great hall. Is Monty correct? Explain your answer.

3.2 Cracking Level 2

For the second level of the Treasure Hunt game, a player must find a hidden treasure on the second floor of the palace. The second floor has rooms for the king's and queen's servants. As in level 1, the computer "thinks" of the floor as a grid and hides the treasure by randomly selecting a grid square. However, notice that the floor of level 2 is *not* a square.

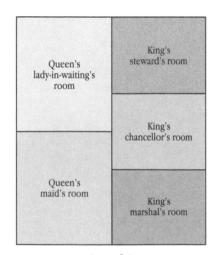

Level 2

Problem 3.2

Answer each question, and explain your reasoning.

A. You have just advanced to level 2 of Treasure Hunt. What is the probability that the treasure is hidden in one of the queen's servants' rooms? In one of the king's servants' rooms?

B. What is the probability that the treasure is hidden in the maid's room? In the steward's room?

C. If you play the second level 100 times, how many times can you expect the treasure to be hidden in one of the queen's servants' rooms? In one of the king's servants' rooms?

D. If you play the second level 100 times, how many times can you expect the treasure to be hidden in the maid's room? In the steward's room?

■ Problem 3.2 Follow-Up

1. You have just advanced to level 2. What is the probability that the treasure is hidden in one of the rooms on the second floor? Explain how you determined your answer.

2. You have just advanced to level 2. What is the probability that the treasure is hidden in the cook's room? Explain how you determined your answer.

As you work on these ACE questions, use your calculator whenever you need it.

Applications

1. The diagram below shows level 3 of the Treasure Hunt game. Before receiving the first clue, a player must guess whether the treasure is in a room used by the king, a room used by the queen, or a room used by the princess. When the treasure is actually located, a player receives bonus points if his or her initial guess was correct.

Level 3

a. Suppose you have just entered level 3. To have the best chance of getting the bonus points, should you guess that the treasure is in one of the king's rooms, one of the queen's rooms, or one of the princess's rooms? Give the reasons for your choice.

b. If you played this level 100 times, how many times would you expect the treasure to be in one of the king's rooms? In one of the queen's rooms? In one of the princess's rooms?

c. If you played this level 100 times, how many times would you expect the treasure to be in the princess's playroom?

In 2–4, use the dartboard shown to answer parts a–c.

2. **3.** **4.**

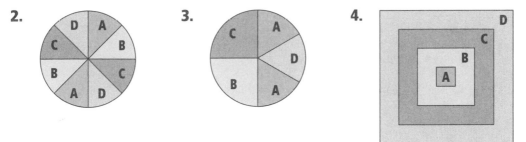

a. If a dart is thrown randomly at the board, what is the probability that it will land in a region marked A? In a region marked B? In a region marked C? In a region marked D?

b. The board is used to play a four-person game. Darts are thrown randomly at the board. Player A receives points when a dart lands in a region marked A, Player B receives points when a dart lands in a region marked B, and so on. Make up a scoring system that would make the game fair.

c. Using your point scheme from part b, what would you expect the score to be after 100 darts have been thrown?

5. Sarah, the designer of the Treasure Hunt game, considered several different floor plans for level 1. Here are two floor plans she rejected. Use these floor plans to answer parts a–d on the next page.

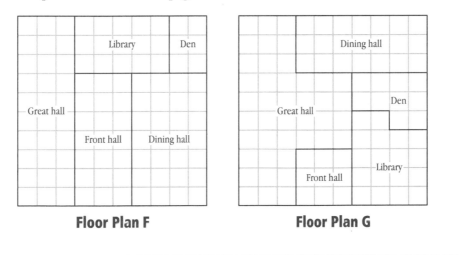

Floor Plan F　　　　　　　**Floor Plan G**

a. If level 1 had floor plan F, what would be the probability that the computer would hide the treasure in the library?

b. If level 1 had floor plan G, what would be the probability that the computer would hide the treasure in the library?

c. If level 1 had floor plan F, how many times out of 100 would you expect the computer to hide the treasure in the library?

d. If level 1 had floor plan G, how many times out of 100 would you expect the computer to hide the treasure in the library?

Connections

6. Sarah tested one of the floor plans from question 5. She kept track of the number of times the treasure was hidden in each room and made a bar graph of the results. Which floor plan do you think she was testing? Explain your reasoning.

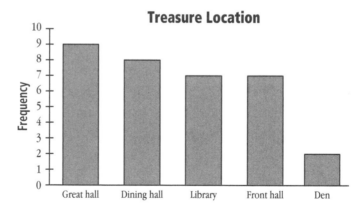

Treasure Location

7. If Sarah had enlarged floor plan F in question 5 by a scale factor of 2 to make a similar floor plan, how would this affect the probabilities?

8. Rich, the programmer of the Treasure Hunt game, tested an early version of the level 1 floor plan. He kept track of the number of times the computer hid the treasure in each room, and he made a line plot of his results:

```
                        X
                        X
           X            X
           X            X
           X            X
           X            X            X
           X            X            X
           X            X            X                         X
           X            X            X            X            X
           X            X            X            X            X
           X            X            X            X            X
        Dining room  Conservatory  Library       Kitchen     Front hall
```

Because of a computer disk error, Rich has no record of the floor plan he was using. Design a floor plan that you would expect to give these data. State the area of each room on your floor plan.

Extensions

9. Create a floor plan for level 4 of the Treasure Hunt game. The floor should have five rooms, and the largest room should have the same area as the other four rooms combined. Label each room, and give its area.

Mathematical Reflections

In this investigation, you solved problems about games of chance in which probabilities were related to area. These questions will help you summarize what you have learned:

1 In games like Treasure Hunt in which probabilities are related to area, how can you tell if two events are equally likely?

2 In the Treasure Hunt game, how can you use the diagram of a level to find the probability that the treasure will be hidden in a particular room?

Think about your answers to these questions, discuss your ideas with other students and your teacher, and then write a summary of your findings in your journal.

Analyzing Two-Stage Games

In the Treasure Hunt game and in games involving spinners and dartboards, you used area to find probabilities. In this investigation, you will learn how to use area in a slightly different way to analyze more situations involving probability.

4.1 Choosing Paths

Kenisha designed a computer game called Deep in the Dungeon. The game pits a player against a computer character named Zark. The game screen is shown below.

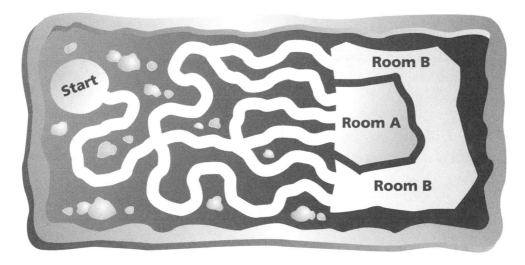

The player puts the treasure in one of the two rooms in the dungeon. Zark begins at "start" and makes his way toward the dungeon, *randomly* selecting a path at each fork. If Zark ends in the room with the treasure, he wins. If he ends in the room without the treasure, the player wins.

A. If you were playing Deep in the Dungeon, in which room would you put the treasure in order to have the best chance of beating Zark? Explain your choice.

B. Work with a partner to find a way to simulate Deep in the Dungeon so it can be played without a computer. Your simulation should be a two-person game. One person should hide the treasure, and the other should play the role of Zark. You will need to figure out a way for Zark to make a random selection at each fork.

C. Play your simulation of Deep in the Dungeon 20 times with your partner. Take turns hiding the treasure and playing Zark. For each game, record the room that Zark ends in.

D. Based on your results from part C, what is the experimental probability that Zark will end in room A? What is the experimental probability that Zark will end in room B?

■ Problem 4.1 Follow-Up

You and your classmates may have found several ways to simulate Deep in the Dungeon in order to find experimental probabilities. How could you determine the theoretical probabilities of Zark ending in each room?

One way to find the theoretical probabilities is by using an *area model.* To make it easier to talk about the game, we'll number the paths as shown below.

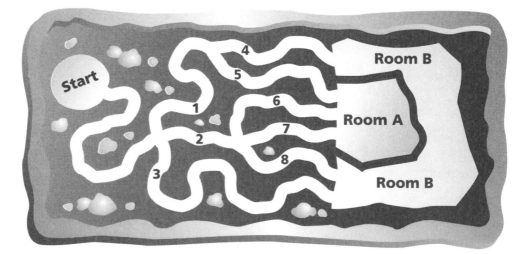

1. Draw a square on your paper. Suppose that the square has an area of 1 square unit, representing a probability of 1. At the first fork, there are three equally likely choices: path 1, path 2, and path 3. Divide and label the square so the areas of the sections represent the probabilities of these three choices.

2. If Zark selects path 1 at the first stage of his journey, he will reach a fork where he must randomly select path 4 or path 5. Subdivide your diagram to represent the probabilities that Zark will choose path 1 and then choose path 4 or path 5.

3. If Zark selects path 2 at the first stage of his journey, he will reach a fork where he must randomly select path 6, path 7, or path 8. Subdivide your diagram to represent the probabilities that Zark will choose path 2 and then choose path 6, path 7, or path 8.

4. On your diagram, color the sections that represent paths leading to room A with one color and the sections that represent paths leading to room B with a second color.

5. What is the theoretical probability that Zark will end in room A? What is the theoretical probability that he will end in room B?

4.2 Finding the Best Arrangement

Brianna and Emmanuel are selected from the studio audience of the Gee Whiz Everyone Wins! game show to play a game. While Emmanuel waits backstage, Brianna is to place two orange marbles and two blue marbles in two identical containers in any way she chooses. After she places the marbles in the containers, Emmanuel will return and select one of the containers at random. Then, without looking, he will reach into the container and pull out a marble. If he draws an orange marble, the friends each win a prize. If he draws a blue marble, or if the container he chooses is empty, the friends do not win anything.

Problem 4.2

A. List all the different ways Brianna can place the four marbles in the two containers.

B. Which arrangement will give Brianna and Emmanuel the best chance of winning? Explain why the arrangement you chose is the best.

C. For the arrangement you chose, what is the probability of drawing an orange marble?

■ Problem 4.2 Follow-Up

1. Which arrangement gives Brianna and Emmanuel the worst chance of winning?

2. Brianna and Emmanuel lost the first game but were given a chance to play a second game. This time Brianna had to place three orange marbles and three blue marbles in three containers. Find the arrangement that gives Emmanuel the best chance of drawing an orange marble.

As you work on these ACE questions, use your calculator whenever you need it.

Applications

1. Kenisha created a new screen for Deep in the Dungeon.

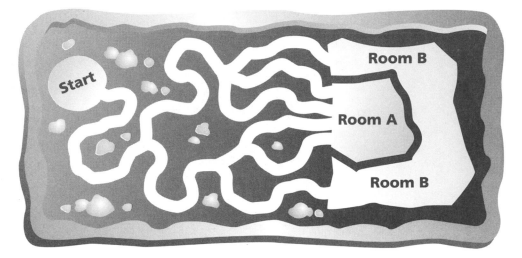

a. If Zark randomly selects a path at each fork, what is the theoretical probability that he will end in room A? In room B?

b. If you played this game 100 times, how many times would you expect Zark to end in room A? In room B?

2. Suppose Brianna (from Problem 4.2) was given three blue marbles and two orange marbles to distribute between the two containers. What arrangement would give Emmanuel the best chance of drawing an orange marble?

3. Suppose Brianna (from Problem 4.2) was given two blue marbles and three orange marbles to distribute between the two containers. What arrangement would give Emmanuel the best chance of drawing an orange marble?

4. Kenisha designed a new version of Deep in the Dungeon with a different arrangement of paths and doors leading into rooms A and B. She made the area model below to analyze the probabilities of landing in each room.

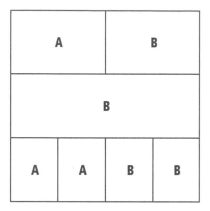

a. For Kenisha's new version, what is the probability that Zark will end up in room A? In room B?

b. Draw a game screen showing the paths, forks, and rooms that represents Kenisha's area model.

Connections

5. The table below shows the results of a survey that asked 100 seniors at Spartan High School the following questions:

- Do you favor a rule that would allow only seniors to drive to school?

- Do you drive to school?

Driving Survey

	Drives to school	Does not drive to school	Row totals
Favors rule	40	30	70
Opposes rule	20	10	30
Column total	**60**	**40**	**100**

a. Based on this survey, what is the probability that a Spartan senior, selected at random, favors the rule?

b. What is the probability that a Spartan senior, selected at random, drives to school *and* favors the rule?

c. What is the probability that a Spartan senior, selected at random, drives to school *or* opposes the rule?

d. Do you think the results of this survey are a good indicator of how all the students at Spartan High School feel about the driving rule? Explain.

6. A bag contains three orange marbles and two blue marbles. You are to choose a marble, return it to the bag, and then choose again.

a. Tell whether each method below is appropriate for finding the possible outcomes of this experiment. If the method is appropriate, explain how you would use it to find the possible outcomes. If the method is not appropriate, explain why.

   i. making a counting tree
   ii. making a list
   iii. using an area model
   iv. making a table or chart

b. If you did this experiment 100 times, how many times would you expect to draw two marbles of the same color?

c. Suppose this experiment were a two-person game in which one player scores if the marbles match, and one player scores if they do not match. Describe a scoring system that would make this a fair game.

Extensions

7. At the school carnival, you are about to play a game using the two spinners below. You get two spins. You may spin each spinner once, or you may spin one of the spinners twice. If you get a red on one spin and a blue on the other spin (the order makes no difference), you win. To have the greatest chance of winning, should you spin spinner A twice, spin spinner B twice, or spin each spinner once? Explain how you got your answer.

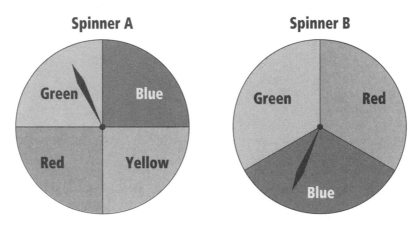

Spinner A

Spinner B

Mathematical Reflections

In this investigation, you analyzed probabilities by dividing the area of a square. These questions will help you summarize what you have learned:

1. In what kinds of situations is it appropriate to find probabilities by dividing the area of a square? Give an example to illustrate your answer.

2. How can you use the area of a square to analyze a probability situation? Use an example to help explain your answer. At each stage, explain how you decide how to divide the square.

   Think about your answers to these questions, discuss your ideas with other students and your teacher, and then write a summary of your findings in your journal.

Expected Value

On April 14, 1993, during half-time of a basketball game between the Chicago Bulls and the Miami Heat, Don Calhoun won 1 million dollars by making a basket from the free-throw line at the opposite end of the court. Don was chosen at random from the audience to attempt the shot as part of a promotional contest. A *Sports Illustrated* article explains:

> The odds against one randomly chosen person given one shot from the opposite foul line and making it are considered astronomical. Scottie Pippen admitted that after practice one day he and Michael Jordan tried to hit the shot but couldn't.*

Not every shot is this difficult to make! In this investigation, you will use a player's free-throw percentage to figure out what is likely to happen in a given free-throw situation.

Shooting the One-and-One

Nicky is playing basketball on her school team this year. In the district finals, the team is 1 point behind with 2 seconds left in the game. Nicky has just been fouled, and she is in a one-and-one free-throw situation. This means that Nicky will try one shot. If she makes the first shot, she gets to try a second shot. If she misses the first shot, she is done and does not get to try a second shot. Nicky's free-throw average is 60%.

*Lisa Bessone, "Sports People: Don Calhoun." *Sports Illustrated*, 26 April 1993, 48.

A. Which of the following do you think is most likely to happen?

- Nicky will score 0 points. That is, she will miss the first shot.
- Nicky will score 1 point. That is, she will make the first shot and miss the second shot.
- Nicky will score 2 points. That is, she will make two shots.

Record what you think before you analyze the situation.

B. Plan a way to simulate this situation. Describe your plan.

C. Use your plan from part B to simulate Nicky's one-and-one situation 20 times. Record the result of each trial.

D. Based on your results, what is the experimental probability that Nicky will score 0 points? That she will score 1 point? That she will score 2 points?

E. Make an area model for this situation, using a 10 by 10 grid. What is the theoretical probability that Nicky will score 0 points? 1 point? 2 points?

F. How do the three theoretical probabilities compare with the three experimental probabilities?

■ Problem 5.1 Follow-Up

1. Suppose Nicky is in a two-shot free-throw situation. This means that she will get a second shot even if she misses the first shot. What is the theoretical probability that Nicky will score 0 points? That she will score 1 point? That she will score 2 points? Explain your reasoning.

2. How do the theoretical probabilities for the one-and-one situation compare to the theoretical probabilities for the two-shot situation?

 Finding Expected Value

In the last problem, you looked at the probabilities of different outcomes of Nicky's one-and-one free-throw situation. You might have been surprised about which outcome is most likely. In this problem, you will look at the number of points Nicky can expect to make each time she is in a one-and-one free-throw situation.

Problem 5.2

Suppose Nicky has a 60% free-throw average and is in a one-and-one free-throw situation 100 times during the season.

A. What total number of points would you expect Nicky to score in these 100 trips to the free-throw line?

B. What would Nicky's average number of points per trip be? This is the **expected value** for this situation.

■ Problem 5.2 Follow-Up

Use Labsheet 5.2 to investigate what is likely to happen in one-and-one situations involving players whose free-throw averages are different from Nicky's. When you have finished the labsheet, use it to help you answer the following questions.

1. How do the probabilities of scoring exactly 1 point in a one-and-one situation compare for 20%, 40%, 60%, and 80% shooters? Describe any pattern you see in the table.

2. In a one-and-one situation, what is the most likely outcome for a 20% shooter? For a 40% shooter? For a 60% shooter? For an 80% shooter? How do these outcomes compare?

3. **a.** Make a graph that shows the average numbers of points a 20% shooter, a 40% shooter, a 60% shooter, and an 80% shooter can expect to make in a one-and-one situation. Use your graph to answer parts b–d.

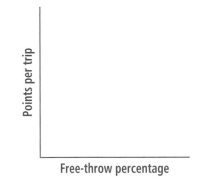

b. How do the expected values compare for a 20% shooter, a 40% shooter, a 60% shooter, and an 80% shooter?

c. Nicky's father noticed that he makes an average of about 1 point whenever he is in a one-and-one free-throw situation. What do you think his shooting percentage is?

d. If Nicky's twin sister Michelle is a 70% shooter, what is her expected value in a one-and-one situation? Check your answer by making an area model.

As you work on these ACE questions, use your calculator whenever you need it.

Applications

1. a. Brian is a 50% free-throw shooter. In a one-and-one free-throw situation, is he most likely to score 0 points, 1 point, or 2 points? Explain your reasoning.

b. Over the long run, what is the average number of points Brian can expect to score per one-and-one situation? That is, what is his expected value?

2. Nicky, a 60% free-throw shooter, is in a two-shot free-throw situation. Remember, this means that she will attempt the second shot no matter what happens on the first shot.

a. Is Nicky most likely to score 0 points, 1 point, or 2 points? Explain your answer.

b. Nicky plans to keep track of her score on two-shot free-throw situations. What average number of points can she expect to score per two-shot situation?

3. Fred and Josephina are experimenting with a new game. They figure out that the probability Fred will win a round is $\frac{1}{3}$, and the probability Josephina will win a round is $\frac{2}{3}$. They decided that to make the game fair Fred should score 3 points when he wins a round, and Josephina should score 2 points when she wins a round.

a. If they play 12 rounds of the game, how many points can Fred expect to score? How many points can Josephina expect to score?

b. How many points per round can each player expect to score? That is, what is the expected value for each player?

c. Is this a fair game? Why or why not?

In 4–6, use the information in this table, which shows free-throw statistics for some of the players on Mr. Luft's basketball team.

Name	Free throws attempted	Free throws made
Gerrit	54	27
David	49	39
Ken	73	45
Alex	60	42

4. Which of the boys listed has the best chance of making his next free throw? Explain your reasoning.

5. a. Alex has just been fouled and is in a one-and-one free-throw situation. What is the probability of each of the following outcomes?

   i. Alex will score 0 points. That is, he will miss the first shot.
   ii. Alex will score 1 point. That is, he will make the first shot and miss the second shot.
   iii. Alex will score 2 points.

b. If Alex is in a one-and-one situation 100 times, how many times would you expect each of the outcomes listed in part a to occur?

c. What is the average number of points you could expect Alex to make per one-and-one situation?

6. a. Suppose Gerrit is in a one-and-one free-throw situation. What is the probability of each of the following outcomes?

      i. Gerrit will score 0 points.
      ii. Gerrit will score 1 point.
      iii. Gerrit will score 2 points.

  b. Suppose Gerrit is in a two-shot free-throw situation. What is the probability of each of the following outcomes?

      i. Gerrit will score 0 points.
      ii. Gerrit will score 1 point.
      iii. Gerrit will score 2 points.

  c. Compare your answers to parts a and b. Explain why the answers to these two questions are not exactly the same.

Connections

7. The Wheel of Fortune® game show uses a large spinner with many sections. At least one section is labeled "bankrupt." If a player spins "bankrupt," she loses her turn and all her money. Luisa created her own version of the Wheel of Fortune spinner so she could play the game with her friends. Her spinner is shown here.

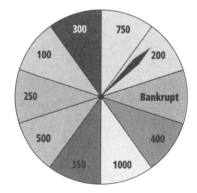

  a. What is the probability that a player who spins this wheel one time will land on bankrupt?

  b. What is the probability that a player who spins this wheel one time will get $500 or more?

  c. Sam just spun the wheel and landed on $350. What is the probability he will land on $350 on his next spin? Explain your reasoning.

8. Wanda, the new Channel 1 weather reporter, said there was a 30% chance of rain on Saturday and a 30% chance of rain on Sunday. It rained both days, and Wanda's station manager is wondering if Wanda really knows how to predict weather.

a. Suppose Wanda had done all the calculations correctly, and according to her data there really was a 30% chance of rain each day. What was the probability that there would be rain on *both* days?

b. Do you think this incident means that Wanda doesn't know very much about predicting weather? Why or why not?

c. Wanda is working on her predictions for the next few days. She uses information from the weather satellite to calculate that there is a 20% chance of rain on Monday and a 20% chance of rain on Tuesday. If she is correct, what is the probability that it will rain on at least one of these days?

9. a. If you roll one number cube two times, what is the probability of getting a factor of 5 both times?

b. If you roll two different number cubes, what is the probability of getting a factor of 5 on both cubes?

c. How do your answers to parts a and b compare? Explain why the answers have this relationship.

10. Mr. Maldonado brought his dog Scout to the vet for a pregnancy test. Since the test gives an accurate prediction only 80% of the time, the vet decides to test Scout twice.

   a. If Scout is pregnant, what is the probability that both tests will say she is *not* pregnant? (It may help to use a 10 by 10 grid to make an area model of this situation.)

   b. If Scout is pregnant, what is the probability that at least one of the tests will indicate that she *is* pregnant?

Extensions

In 11 and 12, use the data about Mr. Luft's basketball team from questions 4–6.

11. What is the probability that Alex will make his next three free throws? Explain your reasoning.

12. David is in a one-and-one free-throw situation. What is the probability that he will make both shots?

13. Regina has worked hard all season and has increased her shooting percentage to 50%. She tells her coach that she would like to be a starter for the rest of the games this season. The coach makes a deal with Regina. At tomorrow's practice, Regina can attempt either to make three shots in a row or to make at least four out of five shots. If Regina is successful, she will start every game for the rest of the season. Which option should Regina choose? Explain your reasoning.

Mathematical Reflections

In this investigation, you learned how to find the average number of points a basketball player could expect to make per trip to the free-throw line. This average is the expected value for the situation. These questions will help you summarize what you have learned:

1 How would you calculate the probability of an outcome that has more than one step? Illustrate your answer by finding the probabilities of the possible outcomes for a 70% free-throw shooter in a one-and-one situation.

2 How would you calculate the expected value for a situation? Illustrate your answer by finding the average number of points per one-and-one situation for a 70% free-throw shooter.

Think about your answers to these questions, discuss your ideas with other students and your teacher, and then write a summary of your findings in your journal.

INVESTIGATION 6

Carnival Games

Next month, Martin Luther King School is having a carnival to raise money for new computer equipment. The students are planning to have a talent show, food stands, and games.

6.1 Drawing Marbles

A committee has been assigned to design and evaluate games for the carnival. The committee will test the games and decide which ones will help the school raise the most money. Julie and Li Fong have designed games that are quite similar.

Julie's idea
A bucket contains four blue marbles and one orange marble. Without looking, a player draws one marble from the bucket, replaces it, and then draws a second marble. If the marble is orange on either draw, the player wins.

Li Fong's idea
A bucket contains four blue marbles and one orange marble. Without looking, a player draws two marbles, one at a time, from the bucket. The player does not replace the first marble before drawing a second marble. If either marble is orange, the player wins.

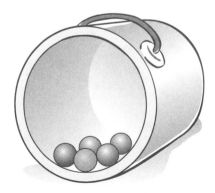

A. Play each game 20 times. Record your results on the board so everyone has access to the class data.

B. Based on the class data, if 100 people play Julie's game, how many people would you expect to win?

C. If 100 people play Li Fong's game, how many people would you expect to win?

■ **Problem 6.1 Follow-Up**

The carnival committee has decided to charge players four 50¢ tickets to play the game. Prizes awarded to the winners will cost the school $5 each.

1. If 100 people play Julie's game, how much money will the school collect? How much money can they expect to pay out in prizes?

2. If 100 people play Li Fong's game, how much money will the school collect? How much money can they expect to pay out in prizes?

3. The committee has decided that it needs only one of the games for the carnival. Which game do you think the carnival committee should use? Explain your choice.

 Choosing the Best Game

Fergus and Judi think they have some interesting ideas for carnival games.

Fergus's idea

Fergus's game is played on a computer. When a player presses the *shift* key, the computer randomly throws two darts, one at a time, at the board shown below. If both darts hit a bonus space, the player wins.

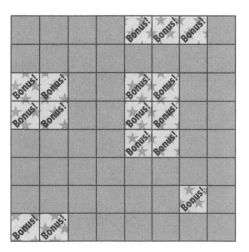

Judi's idea

A player tosses a coin four times. If the player gets three or four heads, he or she wins.

> ### Problem 6.2
>
> **A.** What is the theoretical probability of winning Fergus's game? Explain how you got your answer.
>
> **B.** What is the theoretical probability of winning Judi's game? Explain how you got your answer.

■ Problem 6.2 Follow-Up

1. The carnival committee decides that Fergus's and Judi's games should cost two 50¢ tickets to play, but they are having a hard time deciding how much to spend on prizes. They want to award the same prize for each game. They want to make a profit, but they want the prize to be enticing. How much money do you think the school should spend for each prize? Explain your reasoning.

2. The committee decides it needs only one of the two games for the carnival. Which game do you think the committee should choose? Explain your reasoning.

3. Jovan suggests a slightly different version of Judi's game. As in Judi's game, a player pays two 50¢ tickets and tosses a coin four times. If the coin lands heads up all four times, the player wins a prize worth $5. If the coin lands heads up exactly three times, the player wins a prize worth $2. How much could the school expect to make if 100 students play Jovan's game?

6.3 Taking a Computer Safari

Scott and Regina designed two versions of a computer game called Safari Outrun for the school carnival. The hero of the game, Illinois Bones, drives on jungle roads. At each intersection, the computer randomly selects the path Illinois will travel. At the end of the journey, Illinois will be in city A or city B.

For each version of the game, Scott and Regina have developed a set of jungle roads and a set of prices and prizes.

Version 1

A player pays six 50¢ tickets to play the game. When the player presses the *shift* key, Illinois's journey begins. If Illinois ends in city A, the player receives a prize worth $2. If Illinois ends in city B, the player receives a prize worth $5.

Map for Version 1

Version 2

A player pays ten 50¢ tickets to play the game. When the player presses the *shift* key, Illinois's journey begins. If Illinois ends in city A, the player does not receive a prize. If Illinois ends in city B, the player receives a prize worth $10.

Map for Version 2

The carnival committee is trying to decide which version of the game to use for the carnival. For each version, answer parts A–D.

A. How much money will the school take in if the game is played 100 times?

B. How much money can the school expect to pay out in prizes if the game is played 100 times?

C. What is the average amount the school will pay out each time the game is played?

D. If the game is played 100 times, will the school make money or lose money?

■ Problem 6.3 Follow-Up

Which version of the game do you think the committee should select for the carnival? Explain your answer.

As you work on these ACE questions, use your calculator whenever you need it.

Applications

1. In the Doubles Game, students can win carnival tickets to spend on games and food. A player pays one ticket to roll two number cubes. If the numbers match, the player wins five tickets. If a player plays this game 20 times, about how many tickets can he or she expect to win or lose? Show how you determined your answer.

2. Rashid's grandmother offers him a weekly allowance for helping her with chores around her home. She decides to make a game of it and offers him two options:

Option 1: Rashid's grandmother will give him $10 a week.

Option 2: Each week Rashid's grandmother will put four $1 bills, one $5 bill, and one $10 bill in a bag. Rashid gets to reach in and draw out two bills. This will be his allowance for the week.

The option Rashid chooses will be the method his grandmother uses to pay him for an entire year. Which plan should Rashid choose? Give mathematical reasons to support your answer.

3. Mr. Fujita hires Tasa to mow his lawn for the summer. When Tasa asks him how much he will pay her, he offers her two options:

Option 1: Mr. Fujita will pay Tasa $10 each time she mows his lawn.

Option 2: Each time Tasa mows Mr. Fujita's lawn, she will roll a pair of number cubes. If the sum on the cubes is 7, Mr. Fujita will pay her $30. If the sum is not 7, he will pay her only $3.

Which option should Tasa choose? Give mathematical reasons to support your answer.

Connections

4. a. Design a circular spinner that has six sections with the specified colors and central-angle measurements.

Section color	Central angle	Point value
yellow	20°	6
white	80°	2
black	95°	1
green	50°	4
red	35°	5
blue	80°	3

central angle

b. What is the probability that the spinner will land in each section?

c. If you spin this spinner 100 times, how many points can you expect to get per spin?

5. a. Create a circular spinner with four sections such that the probability of landing in each section is as follows:

red: 10%   yellow: 30%   blue: 45%   white: 15%

b. If you spin this spinner 500 times, how many times can you expect it to land in each section?

6. In the Funny Money game, players spin the spinner shown at right and win the indicated amount in play money. The play money can be used to purchase small prizes at the game store.

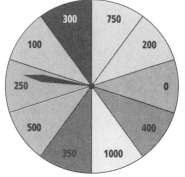

    a. If this game is played 100 times, how much play money can the school expect to pay out?

    b. What is the average payoff per spin?

Extensions

7. In the Rolling for Tickets game, players bet carnival tickets to try to win more tickets to spend on food and games. A player chooses an integer from 1 to 6 and bets as many tickets as he chooses on that number. The player then rolls three number cubes. If the player's number appears on exactly one cube, the player gets his tickets back. If the number appears on exactly two cubes, the player gets twice the number of tickets he bet. If the number appears on all three cubes, the player gets three times the number of tickets he bet.

    a. How many outcomes are there when three number cubes are rolled?

    b. How many ways are there to roll a specific double (such as two 1s or two 2s)? Do not count triples, or getting three of a kind.

    c. What is the probability that exactly two cubes will match? That three cubes will match?

    d. If a player repeatedly bets two tickets on the number 6, what will be the average payoff per roll? Explain how you found this average and what it means in this problem.

8. Della is chosen as a contestant on the Gee Whiz Everyone Wins! game show. The host gives her two red marbles, two green marbles, and two yellow marbles. He tells Della that she may put the marbles into two identical cans in any arrangement she chooses. While Della is blindfolded, the host may change the position of the cans, but he may not change the arrangement of the marbles in the cans. Della will then select a can at random and draw out a marble. If she draws a red marble, she will win a prize. How should Della arrange the marbles so she has the best chance of drawing a red marble?

9. Natasha designed a spinner game for the carnival. The spinner has 38 congruent sections, 18 orange, 18 blue, and 2 white. A player bets play money on orange or blue. If the spinner stops on the color the player has bet on, the player wins double the money bet. If the spinner lands on any other color, the player loses.

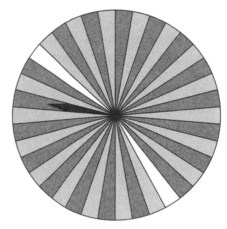

  a. What is the probability that a player will lose on one spin of the wheel?

  b. If a player bets $10 in play money on each spin, what is the average amount of money the player can expect to win or lose per spin of the wheel?

10. a. Curt has been practicing free throws. He has made 60% of his free throws during his practice sessions. The coach says that if Curt makes three free throws in a row, he can start Saturday's game. What is the probability that Curt will make three free throws in a row and start Saturday's game?

  b. Curt has a difficult time making three free throws in a row. The coach tells him to instead try making three out of four shots. What is the probability that Curt will make at least three out of four shots?

Mathematical Reflections

In this investigation, you evaluated potential carnival games. You were interested in the amount of money the school could expect to pay out if the games were played many times. These questions will help you summarize what you have learned:

1 Suppose the principal wants to make sure the school won't lose money at the carnival. How would you explain to the principal how the long-term average of each game, or the expected value, can be computed? Use an example to clarify your explanation.

2 How can expected value help you make decisions in situations involving probabilities and payoffs? Use an example if it helps you to explain your thinking.

Think about your answers to these questions, discuss your ideas with other students and your teacher, and then write a summary of your findings in your journal.

Analyzing Sequences of Outcomes

There are many actions that have exactly two equally likely outcomes. For example, when you toss a coin you may get a head or a tail. When a baby is born, it may be a boy or a girl. In this investigation, you will explore probabilities in situations involving a sequence of actions, each with two equally likely outcomes. For example, if you toss a coin twice, you may get head/head, head/tail, tail/head, or tail/tail. If a woman has two children, she may have two boys, two girls, a girl and then a boy, or a boy and then a girl.

7.1 Counting Puppies

Scout, Mr. Maldonado's Labrador retriever, is about to have puppies. Mr. Maldonado plans to sell the puppies.

Did you know?

Labrador retrievers are the second most popular dog in the world after cocker spaniels. Labrador retrievers make especially good guide dogs for blind people because they are smart and hardworking. In fact, the guide dog who holds the record for length of service to the blind—14 years, 8 months—is Cindy-Cleo, a Labrador retriever from Tel Aviv, Israel.

Source: *The Guinness Book of Records 1994.* Ed. Peter Matthews. New York: Facts on File, 1993.

Problem 7.1

The vet thinks Scout will have four puppies.

A. List all the possible combinations of female and male puppies Scout might have. Assume that for each puppy, a male and a female are equally likely.

B. Is Scout more likely to have four male puppies, or two male puppies and two female puppies? Explain your reasoning.

C. Is Scout more likely to have four male puppies, or a female puppy, a male puppy, a female puppy, and a male puppy, in that order? Explain your reasoning.

■ Problem 7.1 Follow-Up

Since female dogs can be bred to produce puppies, female puppies generally sell for more money than male puppies. Mr. Maldonado plans to sell Scout's female puppies for $250 each and her male puppies for $200 each. How much money can he expect to make for a litter of four puppies?

7.2 Guessing Answers

Have you ever forgotten to study for a quiz and had to guess at the answers? If you take a true-false test and guess on every question, what are your chances of getting every question right?

The following is a true-false quiz about animals. It is written in a secret code.

Animal Olympics Quiz

Tell whether each statement is true or false.

1. [secret code symbols]

2. [secret code symbols]

3. [secret code symbols]

4. [secret code symbols]

Take the Animal Olympics true-false quiz. How did you decide whether to answer true or false on each item?

Below are the results from two classes who took the test. Everyone guessed on every question.

TTFT	TFTF	TTTT	FTFF	FFTF	TFTF
FFTT	TTFF	TFTT	TTTF	FFTT	FFTF
TFFT	FFTT	TFTF	FTFT	TFFF	FTFF
FFFF	FTTF	FTTT	TFFF	FFFT	FFTF
TFFF	FTTT	FTTF	FFFT	TFTF	TTTF
TFTT	FTTF	TFFF	TTFF	FFTT	TFTF
TTFF	FTFT	TFFF	FTFT	TTTF	FTTT
TTFT	FFFT	TFFT	TFFF	FTTF	TFTT
TTTF	FFFF	FFTT	FFTF	TFTF	TFFT
TTTT	FFFT	FTFF	TTTT	TFFT	FFFF

Problem 7.2

Your teacher will give you the correct answers for the quiz.

A. Using the data above, what is the experimental probability that someone who guesses every answer will get all four answers right?

B. What is the experimental probability that someone who guesses every answer will get exactly three answers right?

C. What is the experimental probability that someone who guesses every answer will get exactly two answers right?

D. What is the experimental probability that someone who guesses every answer will get exactly one answer right?

E. What is the experimental probability that someone who guesses every answer will get no answers right?

■ Problem 7.2 Follow-Up

To figure out the theoretical probability of guessing the correct answer to zero, one, two, three, or all four questions, you need to figure out how many ways you can guess right or wrong on a four-question true-false quiz.

1. Use a counting tree to find all the combinations of right and wrong answers for a four-question true-false quiz. Use R to mean "right" and W to mean "wrong." For example, RRRR means all the answers are right, and RRRW means that the first three answers are right and the last answer is wrong.

2. How many right-wrong combinations are there on a four-question true-false quiz?

3. If you guess every answer to a four-question true-false quiz, are you more likely to get exactly two answers right or exactly three answers right? Explain your reasoning.

4. If you guess every answer to a four-question true-false quiz, are you more likely to get the first answer wrong and the last three answers right or to get the first two answers wrong and the last two answers right? Explain your reasoning.

5. Jim says that the probability of getting three answers right is the same as the probability of getting the first answer wrong and the last three answers right. Is he correct? Explain your reasoning.

6. When your class took the quiz, what was the average number of correct answers?

7. Will's teacher gives weekly four-question true-false quizzes. The questions on the quizzes are worth 25 points each. If Will guesses on every question of every quiz he takes, what average score can he expect on his quizzes?

8. a. How does the probability of answering four questions correctly on the quiz compare to the probability that Scout will have four female puppies?

b. How does the probability of answering two questions correctly on the quiz compare to the probability that Scout will have two female puppies?

c. Explain your answers to parts a and b.

As you work on these ACE questions, use your calculator whenever you need it.

Applications

1. It costs six tickets to play the Toss-a-Coin game at the school carnival. For each turn, a player tosses a coin three times. If the coin lands heads up two or more times in a turn, the player wins ten tickets to spend on food and games.

   a. If Ben plays the game 80 times, how many tickets can he expect to win or lose?

   b. What is the average number of tickets Ben can expect to win or lose per turn?

2. **a.** If you toss three coins at the same time, would the probability of getting three heads be the same as or different from the probability of getting three heads when you toss one coin three times in a row? Explain your reasoning.

   b. If you toss three coins and get three tails, what is the probability you will get three tails the next time you toss the three coins? Explain your reasoning.

3. Suppose the vet thinks Scout (from Problem 7.1) will have a litter of five puppies. How much money can Mr. Maldonado expect to make from selling the puppies?

4. **a.** If there were five questions on the Animal Olympics quiz instead of four, what would be the probability of guessing the correct answer to all five questions? Explain your reasoning.

   b. Suppose there were ten questions on the quiz. What do you think the probability of guessing the correct answer to all ten questions would be? Explain your reasoning.

5. How is finding the probability of getting different combinations of heads and tails the same as, or different from, finding the probability of different combinations of male and female puppies in a litter or right and wrong answers on a true-false test?

Connections

6. If you studied the *How Likely Is It?* unit, you learned about the genetics involved in tongue-curling ability. Recall that every person has a combination of two tongue-curling alleles—TT, Tt, or tt—where T is the dominant tongue-curling allele, and t is the recessive non-tongue-curling allele. A person with at least one T allele will be able to curl his or her tongue.

Ken figured out that his tongue-curling alleles are tt and his wife Diane's alleles are Tt. He made this table to help him determine the possible outcomes for their children.

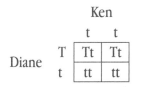

The table shows that the possible combinations are Tt, Tt, tt, and tt. This means that each of Ken and Diane's children has a 50% chance of being able to curl his or her tongue.

a. If Ken and Diane have two children, what is the probability that both of the children will be able to curl their tongues? Make a counting tree to help you answer this question.

b. If Ken and Diane have four children, what is the probability that *none* of the children will be able to curl their tongues?

c. If Ken and Diane have four children, what is the probability that only the *oldest* child will be able to curl his or her tongue?

7. On Thursday, Waldo, the weather reporter for
Channel 6 News, said there was a 50% chance
of rain on Friday, a 50% chance of rain on
Saturday, and a 50% chance of rain on Sunday.
The station manager is upset because it rained
all three days!

    a. Based on Waldo's predictions, what was the
probability that it would rain all three days?

    b. Do you think Waldo's predictions might have been right even though it rained
all three days? Explain your reasoning.

    c. If the chances of rain were actually 40% for Saturday and Sunday, what was
the probability that it would rain both days? Explain your answer.

Extensions

8. Fill-in-the-Blanks is a two-person game. Each player rolls a number cube three
times. After each roll, the player must write the resulting number in one of the
three blanks below. The player who makes the highest three-digit number wins.

___ ___ ___

    a. What is the greatest possible three-digit number a player can get?

    b. What strategies would you use to play the game? Explain your reasoning.

    c. If the blank in which each number is written is chosen randomly, what
is the probability that the greatest possible number will be obtained?

9. Brett invented a game that is played on the number line. At the start of a turn, a player places a marker on 0. The player tosses a penny and moves his marker one unit to the right if the penny lands heads up and one unit to the left if it lands tails up. The player's score for a turn is the number the marker is on after three tosses.

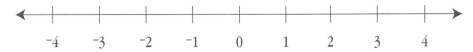

a. What scores are possible after one turn (three tosses)?

b. If Brett changes his game so that a turn consists of four tosses, what scores would be possible after one turn?

10. The largest hamster litter on record consisted of 26 babies. Suppose a hamster has 26 babies. Assume that for each baby, a female and a male are equally likely. What is the theoretical probability that all 26 babies will be male? Explain your reasoning.

11. Mindy is taking a ten-question true-false test. She forgot to study, so she is guessing at the answers.

a. What is the probability that Mindy will get all the answers correct?

b. What is the probability that Mindy will get at least nine answers correct?

12. a. If you toss six pennies, what is the probability that you will get two heads and four tails?

b. If you toss six pennies, what is the probability that you will get four heads and two tails?

Mathematical Reflections

In this investigation, you looked at probabilities for situations involving a sequence of actions, each with two equally likely outcomes. These questions will help you summarize what you have learned:

1 Describe five different situations in which there are two equally likely outcomes.

2 Tossing a coin three times is an example of a situation involving a sequence of three actions, each with two equally likely outcomes.

a. Think of another situation that involves a series of three actions, each with two equally likely outcomes. Make a counting tree to find every possible combination of outcomes.

b. Write a question about your situations that can be answered by using your tree.

3 As you increase the number of questions on a true-false test, what happens to the total number of possible outcomes? Use a specific example, such as the difference between a three-question test and a four-question test, to show what you mean.

Think about your answers to these questions, discuss your ideas with other students and your teacher, and then write a summary of your findings in your journal.

The Carnival Game

This project requires you to use the mathematics you have studied in several units, including this one. In this design project, you will work with a group to create a game for a school carnival and to test your game. Then, you will write a report to the carnival committee about your game.

Step 1: Design a Carnival Game

You can design a new game or redesign one of the games you analyzed in this unit. When you design your game, keep these guidelines in mind:

- The game should make a profit for the school running the carnival.
- The game should be easy to set up and use at a school carnival. It should not require expensive equipment to make or maintain.
- The game should take a relatively short time to play.
- The rules for the game should be easily understood by people your age.

Step 2: Test Your Game

After your group has drafted a game design, you need to decide whether the game you have designed is reasonable for a school carnival and will make a profit. Then, you will need to try out your game. Your group should play the game several times until you feel confident that you can predict what will happen in the long run. Keep track of your trials, and include that information in your report.

Step 3: Submit Your Game Design to the Carnival Committee

Once you are satisfied that your carnival game is reasonable, prepare to submit your game design. Your submission to the committee should include two things: a model or a scale model of the game, and a written report.

Create a Model or a Scale Model

With your group, prepare a model or a scale model of the game. If your group builds a scale model instead of an actual model, give the scale factor from the scale model to the actual game.

You can either construct the model out of similar material that you would use for the actual game, or you can prepare scale drawings of the game. If your group makes drawings, be sure to include enough views of your game so that anyone could look at the drawings and construct the game.

With your model, include a set of rules that explains how the game is played, how much it costs to play, how a player wins, and how much a player wins. Explain how the game would make a profit.

Write a Report

Write a report about your game to the carnival committee. Assume that the carnival committee is composed of teachers in the building (not just mathematics teachers), parents, and other students. Your report should include the following:

- *The probability of winning the game.* Give the experimental probability of winning the game that you found from playing the game several times. If possible, give the theoretical probability as well. For some games, such as tossing coins or drawing blocks from a container, finding the theoretical probability of winning is easy. For others, finding the theoretical probability may be too difficult. If you don't give the theoretical probability of winning for your game, explain why you did not.

- *The amount collected and expected payout per game.* Tell how much money the school will collect and how much they could expect to pay out if the game is played many times. Show how you determined these amounts.

- *An explanation of why your game should be chosen.* Explain why the game is worth having in the carnival and why you think people would want to play it.

Looking Back and Looking Ahead

Unit Reflections

The problems in this unit extended your knowledge of probability to several strategies for finding and interpreting *experimental* and *theoretical probabilities*. You used simulations to gather experimental data, *counting trees* and other listing techniques to find all of the possible outcomes in a problem situation, and *area models* in which probabilities are shown as parts of a whole rectangle or circle.

Using Your Probability Reasoning—To test your understanding and skill with probability ideas and strategies, consider the following problem situations.

1. *Sydney has a homework problem asking for designs of two dartboards that match these conditions:*

   - *The probability of landing in region A is 30%.*
   - *The probability of landing in region B is 25%.*
   - *The probability of landing in region C is 20%.*
   - *The remaining space on the dartboard is region D.*

   a. Draw a square dartboard that meets the given conditions.

   b. Draw a circular dartboard that meets the given conditions.

   c. For each dartboard, what is the probability that a dart will

      i. land in region D?

      ii. land in a region other than D?

      iii. *not* land in Region A?

2 *Glenda and Jim are playing the Match/No Match game. On each turn, the players spin the two spinners shown below. Player A scores 1 point if the spins match, and Player B scores 1 point if they do not match.*

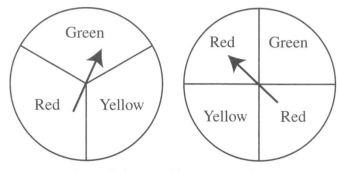

   a. Use a counting tree to show all the possible outcomes for this game.

   b. What is the theoretical probability of getting a match?

   c. What is the theoretical probability of getting a non-match?

   d. Is this a fair game? If you think the game is fair, explain why. If you think the game is not fair, explain how you could change the rules to make it fair.

3 *Kali and Tony designed a new computer game. They programmed the game so the probability that a player will win is $\frac{1}{4}$ on each turn. If the player wins, the score increases by four points. If the player loses, two points are deducted from the score.*

   a. If Monte plans to play 12 rounds of the game, how many points can he expect to score?

   b. How many points per round can Monte expect to win or lose?

   c. Is this a fair game? If not, how would you change the points won or lost so that it would be a fair game?

Explaining Your Reasoning—When you use mathematical calculations or diagrams to solve a problem or make a decision, it is important to justify your reasoning. Answer these questions about your work.

1. What does it mean to say that the probability of some event is $\frac{1}{2}$ or $\frac{2}{3}$ or $\frac{5}{8}$?

2. How are experimental and theoretical probabilities for an event related to each other?

3. Explain and illustrate with a specific example how you could use each of these strategies to analyze probabilities.

    a. Counting trees   **b.** Area models

4. What does it mean to find the expected value of a chance activity with numerical outcomes? Give three examples of problems in this unit for which you had to compute expected value.

You will almost certainly meet this unit's ideas about probability in future study and problem solving in mathematics, science, and games of chance. These are the basis of statistical reasoning that will be developed in the *Connected Mathematics* unit *Samples and Populations* and in areas as diverse as the biology of genetics and the payoffs in state lotteries and local fund-raisers.

Glossary

counting tree A diagram used to determine the number of possible outcomes in a probability situation. The number of final branches is equal to the number of possible outcomes. The counting tree below shows all the possible outcomes for randomly choosing a yellow or red rose and then a white or pink ribbon. The four possible outcomes are listed in the last column.

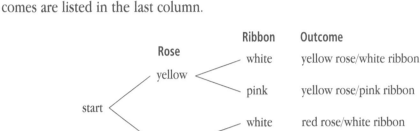

equally likely events Two or more events that have the same probability of occurring. For example, when you toss a fair coin, heads and tails are equally likely; each has a 50% chance of happening.

event A set of outcomes. For example, when two coins are tossed, getting two matching coins is an event consisting of the outcomes HH and TT.

expected value, long-term average The average payoff over many trials. For example, suppose you are playing a game with two number cubes in which you score 2 points when a sum of 6 is rolled, 1 point for a sum of 3, and 0 points for anything else. If you were to roll the cubes 36 times, you could expect to roll a sum of 6 about five times and a sum of 3 about twice. This means that you could expect to score $(5 \times 2) + (2 \times 1) = 12$ points for 36 rolls, an average of $\frac{12}{36} = \frac{1}{3}$ point per roll. This is the expected value of a roll.

experimental probability A probability that is determined through experimentation. For example, you could find the experimental probability of getting a head when you toss a coin by tossing a coin many times and keeping track of the outcomes. The experimental probability would be the ratio of the number of heads to the total number of tosses, or trials. Experimental probabilities are used to predict behavior over the long run.

fair game A game in which each player has the same chance of winning. The probability of winning a two-person fair game is $\frac{1}{2}$. An unfair game can be made fair by adjusting the scoring system, or the payoffs. For example, suppose you play a game in which two fair coins are tossed. You score when both coins land heads up; otherwise, your opponent scores. The probability that you will score is $\frac{1}{4}$, and the probability that your opponent will score is $\frac{3}{4}$. To make the game fair, you might adjust the scoring system so that you receive 3 points each time you score and your opponent receives 1 point when he or she scores.

outcome A possible result of an action. For example, when a number cube is rolled, the possible outcomes are 1, 2, 3, 4, 5, and 6.

probability A number between 0 and 1 that describes the likelihood that an event will occur. For example, a fair number cube is rolled. There is one way out of six possibilities that a 2 can be rolled, so the probability of rolling a 2 is $\frac{1}{6}$. The probability of a certain event is 1, while the probability of an event that cannot occur is 0.

random events Events whose outcomes are uncertain when viewed individually, but which may exhibit a predictable pattern when observed over many trials. For example, when you roll a fair number cube, you have no way of knowing what the next roll will be, but you do know that, over the long run, you will roll each number on the cube about the same number of times.

theoretical probability A probability obtained by analyzing a situation. If all the outcomes are equally likely, you can find a theoretical probability of an event by listing all the possible outcomes and then finding the ratio of the number of outcomes in which you are interested to the total number of outcomes. For example, there are 36 possible equally likely outcomes (number pairs) when two fair number cubes are rolled. Of these, six have a sum of 7, so the probability of rolling a sum of 7 is $\frac{6}{36}$, or $\frac{1}{6}$.

Index